Richard Salter Storrs

John Wycliffe and the First English Bible

An Oration

Richard Salter Storrs

John Wycliffe and the First English Bible
An Oration

ISBN/EAN: 9783337098322

Printed in Europe, USA, Canada, Australia, Japan

Cover: Foto ©Lupo / pixelio.de

More available books at **www.hansebooks.com**

AND

THE FIRST ENGLISH BIBLE

AN ORATION

BY

RICHARD S. STORRS, D.D., LL.D

NEW YORK
ANSON D. F. RANDOLPH & COMPANY
900 BROADWAY, COR. 20th STREET
1880

With a view to commemorate the services of the eminent Reformer, to whom, more than to any other person, the world is indebted for the first translation of the Holy Bible into the English language, the Board of Managers of the American Bible Society invited the Rev. Dr. Richard S. Storrs to deliver a public Oration upon the life and work of John Wycliffe. In compliance with that invitation the following discourse was pronounced in the Academy of Music, New York, on the evening of Thursday, December 2d, 1880, before a very large assembly, representing all the branches of the Christian Church which are united in the work of circulating the Holy Scriptures among all nations, through the agency of the American Bible Society.

Author's Note.

On account of the length of the following discourse, portions of it were omitted in the delivery, which are retained in the printed copies.

Occasional foot-notes have been added, usually to supply support or illustration to statements in the text, sometimes to suggest to those interested by the subject, and wishing to make further inquiry about it, such books, or parts of books, commonly accessible, as will be likely to afford the readiest assistance.

ORATION.

Mr. President: Ladies, and Gentlemen:

On the left bank of the Rhine, on the site of the ancient Roman camp, afterward an imperial colony, which is associated in history with Tiberius and Germanicus, with Agrippina, mother of Nero, and with the early fame of Trajan, has been recently completed a magnificent work of religion and of art, of which more than six centuries have witnessed the progress. After delays immensely protracted, after such changes in society and government, in letters, arts, and in prevalent forms of religious faith, that the age which saw its solemn foundation has come to seem almost mythical to us, by contributions in which peoples have vied with princes, and in which separated countries and communions have gladly united, the cathedral of Cologne has been carried to its superb consummation, and the last finial has been set upon the spires which at length fulfil the architect's design.

Attendant pomps, of imperial pageantry, were naturally assembled on such an occasion; but they can have added no real impressiveness to the structure itself, with its solid strength matching its lofty and lovely proportions, the vast columns of the nave lifting upon them plume-like pillars, the majestic choir, of stone and glass, with its soft brilliance and exquisite tracery, beautiful as a poet's dream, the soaring open-work of the spires, absorbing and moulding hills of rock in their supreme and ethereal grace. It seems impossible not to apply to it the words which Gibbon applied to St. Peter's: "the most glorious structure that ever has been applied to the use of religion."* It is impossible not to rejoice that the common sentiments of beauty and of worship survive the changes of civilization, so that distant centuries join hands in the work now finished and crowned, and the completion of this grandest of cathedrals in Northern Europe fitly attracts the attention of Christendom.

It is a work at first sight insignificant in comparison with this, which we have met to commemorate this evening: the translation of the Scriptures into the common English tongue, begun by John Wycliffe five centuries ago, and brought to completeness in these recent days by the hands of English and American scholars. It may seem that the vision of the majestic cathedral is too stately and splendid to be set in front of a story so simple, and in parts so familiar, as that which we are here to recall. But I think it will appear that the work which we celebrate

---

* "Decline and Fall," Vol. VIII., p. 466.

is the nobler of the two; that from all the costly and skillful labors, now completed on the banks of the Rhine, we arise to this: even as there one advances to the altar, supreme in its significance, through the decorated doorways, along the vast nave, and under the rhythmic and haughty arches. To us, at least, the voice of God becomes articulate through the book; while the building only shows us the magnificent achievement of human genius, patience, and wealth, bringing to Him their unsurpassed tribute.

It is, however, a very plain tale which I have to tell; and the interest of it must lie in its substance, not in any ornaments of language or of thought associated with it. In order to tell or to hear it aright we have to recall many things which lie back of it, which alone can set it clearly before us.

That the governing authorities in the Christian world should have ever refused to the revered Scriptures, on which the common faith was founded, the widest distribution in the various languages spoken by the peoples holding that faith, is a fact so peculiar that we easily ascribe it to a crafty ambition or an arrogant self-will, and dismiss it as thus superficially explained. We forget how deeply rooted it was in an immense system of thought and of government, and through what silent organic processes it came to evolution into custom and rule.

Of course it contradicted the earlier usage and plan of the Church. The Hebrew and Chaldaic Scriptures had been written in the dialects familiar to the people among whom and for whom they were prepared, before and after the Eastern captivity. When Greek became a customary speech, with those dispersed in distant cities, the Alexandrian version of these Scriptures was made; and, as we know, in the time of the Master, it was commonly read and reverently expounded by the teachers of religion, as it afterward long continued in use with Christian converts.

The Evangelists and Apostles, after the Lord had left the earth, wrote accounts of his life, with arguments of doctrine, precepts, promises, and prophetic admonitions, in the language familiar to themselves and their disciples—the vigorous, copious, Hellenistic Greek, to which the commerce of the time had given wide distribution, while the Septuagint had given it consecration. They sought to reach not scholars only, or lettered persons, but all peoples who shared in the general culture, and all classes of people, with the writings upon which their souls were engaged, and in which they felt themselves moved and helped by the Divine Spirit. The preference of St. Paul was shared by all; it was his preference when dictating or tracing the large and slow characters, as well as when preaching: "I had rather speak five words with my understanding, that by my voice I might teach others also, than ten thousand words in an unknown tongue." And it was by these Scriptures, in the language which then had chief currency in the world, and in which the Roman Law itself was subsequently written, that the knowledge of Him in whom is the light and the hope of mankind was soon distributed over vast spaces.

Yet again, as subsequent need arose that the Scriptures be put into other languages, to reach more directly remoter peoples, this was done without opposition, with encouragement indeed, of Church authorities. So came the early Latin versions, for use in North Africa or in Italy, in the second century. So came the later translation of Jerome, from the originals, which became afterward practically the Bible of Western Christendom. The Syriac version, which before the end of the second century carried the Scriptures to the Euphrates, followed by others in the same tongue; the Thebaic, and Memphitic, which made them equally at home on the Nile; the Æthiopic, of the fourth century; the Gothic, of the same period, made by Ulphilas; the Armenian, of the fifth century; the Arabic, Persian, and all the others, to the Sclavonic of the ninth century, reveal the same impulse of wisdom and zeal, as all are designed to bring the quickening Word of God into contact with those to whom the Hebrew and the Greek were not familiar. Certainly, for centuries after the Ascension, it would have seemed as absurd to restrain the Scriptures to languages not understood by the people, as it would have been on the crest of Olivet to thrust veils of darkness beneath the cloud which received the

Lord, and to leave the disciples uncertain of His glory. The latest and fiercest Roman persecution, under Galerius and Diocletian, aimed especially to destroy the Church by destroying its sacred and life-giving books.

Perhaps nothing else more signally shows the novel and alien character of the power which in subsequent centuries grew up in Christendom than does the fact that it wholly departed from these primitive traditions, and wrought against them, of settled purpose, with restless energy, by an instinct of its nature. I need not repeat the story of its rise. I may only remind you how its portentous physical development allied itself naturally with a peculiar doctrine and temper, as the primitive popular church-organization, whose picture is ineffaceably preserved on immortal records, gave place by degrees to the splendid and vast imperial system, enthroned in the capital which still fascinates the fancy and awes the imagination of the cultivated world, having prelates for its princes, and extending its sway more widely over Europe than had the Empire which it followed and surpassed.

This system was by no means wholly for evil. Undoubtedly, certain needs of the time found in it their special supply, and important benefits to mediæval society are fairly ascribed to it. It held the tumultuous populations of Europe to some degree of civilized order, amid stupendous changes and strifes, the fall of the Empire, the in-rush of barbarians from wood and waste, the utter breaking up of the ancient governing order of things. When the sovereignty of force threatened to become the law of the planet, it asserted the supremacy of the spiritual order over the secular, in Divine adjustments. It built monasteries, for those who sought equally seclusion and society, with industry, study, and the worship of God. It defended those monasteries by sanctions of religion, which even breasts that wore mail, and hands that held lances, had to regard. It preserved in their libraries the scattered remains of the classical literature, as well as the Scriptures; and by the labor of monks it multiplied copies of what thus was preserved, and transmitted them to us. It built cathedrals, and abbey-churches, vast poems in stone, which inspire the fond admiration of Christendom by their melodious and consecrated beauty. It established universities, for the teaching of its doctrines, but with an inevitably wider effect on the culture of mankind. It proclaimed the "truce of God," to mitigate and restrain, where it might not prohibit, the savage and sanguinary combats of men. It loosed the bonds of human slavery from multitudes of victims, and honorably refused to recognize distinctions of bond or free among its officers. It made the stoutest baron tremble, in the ecstasy of his passion, before the invisible energy of the curse with which it could blast his cruelty or his lust. Sometimes, indeed, upon kings themselves, when their tyranny was most fierce, it laid a hand far heavier than theirs, and held them in enforced and reluctant submission.

Surely it was something to have peoples thus taught that there was an authority higher than of princes, a right more imperative, a tribunal more august. And I cannot but think it beyond dispute that a power was exerted from the banks of the Tiber, in different directions, between the fifth and the fourteenth centuries, to restrain some of the most malign evils, and encourage some of the germs of good, in that fateful and perilous time. It taught the nations, however obscurely, their Christian relationship to each other, and prepared the way for International Law; while the out-ranging missions of Europe, for the conquest of the heathenism which still girt it about, took steadiness, ardor, and a regulating order, from this vast Church authority, and smote with more effective impact upon the mighty ring of darkness.

The whole system which thus took the place in Europe of the earlier, simpler Christian economy, and whose existence was for many generations the sovereign fact in the history of the Continent, appears now an anachronism, as truly as tournaments, feudal keeps, or iron helmets. The terrible crozier, before which baton and lance went down in fear, has no more place for such use in our times than has scale-armor, or the Genoese cross-bow. But then it had a great purpose to serve; and one who discerns the salutary ends which the Church as imperially organized accomplished, may admire anew the patience and the wisdom whose silent grasp no power eludes, and which even man's wrath at last must praise.

But now it is obvious that with this system of organization had grown up one of doctrine and of worship, and had been developed spiritual tendencies, whose effects were widely and dangerously evil; against which Christians had at length absolutely to rebel, to maintain or regain the Gospel of Christ. And here it was that the Scriptures met their determined antagonist.

The solemn setting apart of men to offices of permanent prerogative and control, in a vast, ancient, and dominating Hierarchy, almost inevitably induced the assumption that the Church was in them, as Louis of France declared himself "the State," and that men must abide in communion with them on peril of losing eternal life. In their view, it had commission, this priestly Church, with affirmative voice to declare and unfold, even to supplement, what was taught in the Scriptures. It had power, as well, to communicate grace, transmitted through it by its Divine Head, on effectual sacraments: giving in baptism the germinant principle of spiritual life; restoring it in penance; nourishing and renewing it in other sacraments, most of all in the Eucharist. It was in orderly development of this system that the very body and blood of the Lord were at last affirmed to be in the wafer[*]—

---

[*] At the Lateran Council, A.D. 1215.

the Infinite in the finite, the personal presence and glory of the Redeemer in material particles; and that thenceforth the chief vehicle of grace to the soul which received it was held to be not the word of the Master, but this figure of bread, over which thaumaturgic words had been spoken, and behind whose accidents was the hidden splendor and life of God's Son.

With this came naturally a form of worship pictorial and spectacular, rather than instructive; an homage paid to the hierarchies above; the increasing adoration of the "Mother of God"; and all the forms of doctrine and practice still presented by the modern representative of the middle-age Christendom. The entire system, in its gradual expansion to its ultimate surprising symmetry and vigor, rises before one in the pages of history as plainly as the chain of the Cordilleras on a recent ample topographical map. It corresponded with the vast politico-religious organization in which it was formulated. It seemed to supply the reason for that; and it wrought, with and through it, with an energy seemingly inexhaustible.

Of course, by its nature, the entire system was profoundly adverse to the popular reading of the Scriptures. It was surely conscious of many things, —in the worship of Saints, or of the Virgin, in the efficacy of sacraments, the traditional functions of prelates or the Pontiff—for which no warrant could be found in the Word, if that did not distinctly contradict them, and foretell their mischiefs. To allow men to search the Scriptures for themselves was practically to suspend the function of the Hierarchy, as the authorized expositor of the Divine teaching. All divisions of opinion might then be apprehended. A man might even come to feel that he had no further need of a priest, as the mediator between Christ and his soul, but could go himself, in sorrow for sin or in petition for favor, to Him whose mind had touched his in the Gospel. It could not, indeed, have seemed inconceivable that an entire scheme of doctrine, based on the idea that faith in the Lord is that which justifies, and that such faith has in it the power of the life everlasting, might thus finally appear in the world. And the whole pontifical organization would be in peril if such an exposition were given to the argument of the Pauline epistles.

It must be observed, too, that what we hold—justly, we think—the evil effects of a long withholding of the Scriptures from the people, came to furnish fresh argument for it. The four-fold significance recognized in those Scriptures could only be discerned by devout and competent spirits. If then it had come to pass, as plainly as it had, that neither intellectual nor spiritual insight was commonly to be found in religious assemblies—that the people who bowed in adoration to images, less graceful than the Greek and less august than the Roman, who trusted in the wood of the Cross, who rang bells in the night to frighten the demons from the air, and who only felt the sanctity of an oath as it had been taken on ancient relics and unauthenticated bones, that these could scarcely be expected to feel the sublime pathos of the gospels, or to follow the excursions of Paul's inspired and rapid reason—all the more was it certain to those in authority that it would be casting pearls before swine, intoxicating weak and unprepared souls with precious cordials, to freely open the Scriptures to all. Undoubtedly often, to devout minds, it seemed a token of reverence for these to keep them apart from ignoble hands; while it seemed equally a tenderness to those who might be seduced, through misconceiving the Word, into dangerous error.

So it came to pass, in no flash of petulant arrogance, by no inexplicable frenzy of councils, but by a logical moral progress, certain and governing, that the early plan of putting the writings in which Christianity was declared to the world into the hand of every reader, for his guidance to the Master, or for his sweeter wisdom and grace, was suspended and antagonized by the later plan of keeping all teaching in the hands of the priesthood, and reserving to a language understood by only the educated class the sacred books. Reverence for these books had preserved them in the monasteries with effectual care. It had caused them to be often transcribed by the monks, to be splendidly ornamented, superbly bound, embossed and enriched with gold and gems, till a copy was almost worth in commerce the price of a castle.* But it had hidden them from the touch of the laity with as jealous a care; and the tendency to that was as unreturning as the steady slip of the stream to the sea. A distinct prohibition of the Scriptures to the people was promulgated at Toulouse, A.D. 1229.† It had been a rule of the Greek Church before. But particular decrees only uttered a rule which lay back of all, and was inherent in the system of thought from which they sprang. As that system became perfected, its tone grew sharper and more imperious. It watched its domains with a vigilance unsleeping. And he who thereafter would place the Scriptures, in a language familiar, before the people, must cross

---

* The Abbot Angilbert gave to the Abbey of St. Riquier, in A.D. 814, a copy of the Gospels, "in letters of gold, with silver plates, marvellously adorned with gold and precious stones." Louis Debonair gave to a monastery at Soissons a copy of the Gospels "written in letters of gold, and bound in plates of the same metal, of the utmost purity." In A.D. 1022 the Emperor presented to the monastery of Monte Casino a copy of the Gospels "covered on one side with most pure gold, and most precious gems, written in uncial characters, and illuminated with gold." Many other like instances of costly copies of the Scriptures, or of parts of them, are noted in monastic records.—*See Maitland's "Dark Ages,"* pp. 205–220.

† "We also forbid the laity to possess any of the books of the Old or New Testament, unless, perhaps, the Psalter or Breviary for the Divine Offices, or the Hours of the Blessed Virgin, some, out of devotion, may wish to have; but that any should have these books translated into the vulgar tongue we strictly forbid [arctissime inhibemus]."

swords with the power which had kings for its vassals, their armies for its troops, and upon the plates of whose alleged supernal armor the fiercest chieftains had shivered their blades.

But now it is also to be observed that against this tendency had been at least occasional resistance, by many of the best among the people, and of the priesthood; and that this had been as manifest as anywhere in that earlier England, which, after a frightful paralysis of its powers, had come, at just the time of Wycliffe, to its incipient resurrection. We have to trace this history, also, to get his work, in its impulse, its meaning, and its fruitful effect, fully before us.

The movements toward a more spiritual faith which at different times had appeared on the Continent—represented in part by the Paulicians, by Claude of Turin, by Peter de Bruys, by Arnold of Brescia, or, more largely, by Waldo and his followers—these seem to have made slight impression on the peoples in England. Their relations with the Continent were not close; and thought passed slowly, in those sluggish times, from one state to another. But among the German peoples themselves, who had conquered Britain, there had been developed at different times a practical tendency toward freedom in religion, and especially toward a more personal and general acquaintance with the Scriptures.

Of course their history, after settling in England, had been very largely one of strife. It startles us to remember that more than one year out of two, in the whole six centuries of their growing domination, had been occupied in struggle: against the preceding inhabitants of the country, among themselves, or against the roving tribes which had followed; while the breaking in of the still pagan Danes, upon the state which was painfully striving toward Christian order, immensely retarded its moral progress. Yet the active and strenuous spirit of the Saxons, after they had accepted the Christianity which Gregory sent, by the Abbot Augustine and his forty monks, had never ceased to work toward better and larger knowledge, and a more secure freedom. The name "Saxon" may not have come, as some have derived it, from the short sword-axe, or "Seax," which they carried;* but the weapon certainly well represented their self-asserting and resolute temper, to which war was familiar, and which sought utility as the prime good in instruments. There was nothing very fine or ethereal about them. They were not distinguished for brightness of fancy, or moral delicacy, or for unusual spiritual insight. But they had a sense of personal right, which was vital and strong, with a certain robust practical intelligence; while they readily received whatever forms of foreign culture they could assimilate.

---

* Thierry seems to accept this : "Saxons, or men with the long knives ; " "Sax, saex, seax, sæx, knife or sword. Handsax, poniard. (Gloss. of Wachter)."—*Nor. Conq.*, Vol. I., p. 9.

They had gained written codes, as one effect of their new religion. They had gained a force from the world at large, to expand and lift the insular spirit. Archbishop Theodore, an Asiatic Greek from Tarsus, in the seventh century brought to Canterbury an extraordinary library, containing Greek authors as well as Latin. He established important schools in the kingdom, and himself taught arithmetic, astronomy, medicine, and divinity. The African Abbot, Adrian, who accompanied him, was of a like spirit; and in less than a century from the landing of the monks, Caedmon of Whitby was reciting to the Abbess Hilda and her scholars the first English song—of Creation, of Judgment, and of what lies between; Aldhelm, of Malmesbury, was inventing the organ, and writing the earliest Latin verse; while the eloquence and the sanctity of Cuthbert seemed to open heaven to the eyes of those to whom he preached. In the following century Offa, the king, not only struck coins and medals, and built an abbey and a palace, but he framed laws to promote Christian morals, drew closer the relations of England to the Continent, and corresponded with Charlemagne, on matters of commerce and education.

Alfred, of the ninth century, by consent of all one of the leading figures in history—not great in opportunity, but great in mental and moral force—is the typical Saxon. He had been upon the Continent, and had there had experience of a higher civilization than existed in England. He sought to assemble learned men at his court, as Grimbald from St. Omer's, and Asser from St. David's. He learned Latin himself, in the intervals of a life crowded with care and thick with battles, that he might open its treasures to others. He translated from it Orosius' History, with additions of his own; Gregory's treatise on the duty of Pastors; Boëthius, on the Consolation of Philosophy; the Ecclesiastical History of Bede, and parts of the writings of St. Augustine. He personally translated parts of the Scripture, and was engaged at his death on a Saxon Psalter. Historians find a striking illustration of the range of his thought in the fact that he sent ambassadors from England to the ancient Christian churches in India. A clearer illustration appears in the fact that he founded schools at Winchester and Oxford—the latter of which has not unreasonably been considered the germ of the later University; that he sought a higher education for girls, as well as for boys; and that he expressed the kingly wish that all the free-born English youth should some time read with correctness and ease the English Scriptures. Athelstane, his grandson, was hardly behind him in his desire to further learning and promote moral welfare; and he also pressed the translation of the Scriptures into the common English speech. The "Durham Book," of Latin gospels, with Saxon glosses interlined, the most beautiful example of Saxon calligraphy, is perhaps of his time.

In spite, therefore, of tides of battle ever rising and slowly receding, a true progress had been realized in England, in the direction of those attainments which have given to the nation its subsequent fame. Men for the time distinguished by their accomplishments began to appear. The Abbot Benedict brought costly books, and works of art, on his return from each of his journeys to Rome.* The Venerable Bede, in the eighth century, found learning, teaching, and writing, as he said, a constant delight.† He learned Greek, as well as Latin, with something of Hebrew, and quoted Plato and Aristotle, as well as Seneca, Cicero, and Virgil. He left forty-five books to attest his industry, on science, philosophy, as well as theology; and is said to have first introduced the use of the Christian era in historical writing. He drew to himself six hundred scholars; and he died, as we know, while engaged in translating the Gospel of John into the stubborn Saxon tongue. Burke calls

---

* "He brought treasures back with him, chiefly books in countless quantities, and of every kind. He was a passionate collector, as has been seen, from his youth. He desired each of his monasteries to possess a great library, which he considered indispensable to the instruction, discipline, and good organization of the community."—*Montalembert*, "*Monks of the West*," Vol. IV., p. 443.

† "Cunctum vitæ tempus in ejusdem monasterii habitatione peragens, omnem meditandis Scripturis operam dedi; atque inter observantiam disciplinæ regularis et quotidianam cantandi in ecclesia curam, semper aut discere, aut docere, aut scribere dulce habui."—*See Giles' "Life of Ven. Bede*," Vol. I., p. lii.

him "the Father of the English learning"; and, though denying him genius, credits him with "an incredible industry, and a generous thirst of knowledge."*

Alcuin, who came later, the friend and instructor of Charlemagne, had been educated at York, where the library collected by Archbishop Egbert was already so rich that he remembered it with delight and regret from his more brilliant Southern home, and longed that "some of its fruits might be placed in the Paradise of Tours." Dunstan, of the tenth century, though of a fiery arrogance of temper, supremely devoted to the Papacy, was also an assiduous student, a designer and painter, a skilful musician, with taste in the arrangement of jewels and the illustration of books, a judge even of embroidery, and fond of rich architecture. The literary eminence of the Saxon clergy was then acknowledged by other nations. The schools, at York, and at Jarrow on the Tyne, were celebrated; and the Anglo-Saxon Chronicle, of the time of Alfred, remains, with the exception of Ulphilas' translation, the most venerable monument of Teutonic prose.

The general moral progress of the nation, though

---

* "Abridg. Eng. Hist." Works, Vol. V., p. 532.

Sharon Turner says of Bede, somewhat extravagantly, that he "collected into one focus all that was known to the ancient world, excepting the Greek mathematicians, and some of their literature and philosophy, which he had not much studied."—"*Hist. Ang. Sax.*," Vol. III., p. 356.

not rapid or signal, appeared thus secure. Industries were multiplied; gardens and orchards began to replace the forests, swamps, and pasture-lands; articles of taste came to be frequent, musical instruments, cups of twisted glass, or of gold or silver, curiously wrought, which were often exported. The walls of churches were hung not unfrequently with pictures and tapestries, and silver candelabra were on the altars. The even-song of the monks at Ely floats to us over the centuries, and the Danish Canute's enjoyment of it has been commemorated in lovely lines by a great English poet.* Woman had relatively a high position in the Saxon communities,†

---

* " A pleasant music floats along the Mere,
From monks in Ely chanting service high,
While-as Canùte, the King, is rowing by:
* * * * *
The Royal Minstrel, ere the choir is still,
While his free barge skims the smooth flood along,
Gives to that rapture an accordant Rhyme."

WORDSWORTH, " Eccl. Sonnet," XXX.

The remaining fragment of this " Rhyme " is said by Turner to be the oldest specimen left of a genuine ballad in the Anglo-Saxon language.—"*Hist. Ang. Sax.*," Vol. III., p. 249.

† " They were allowed to possess, to inherit, and to transmit landed property; they shared in the social festivities; they were present at the Witenagemot and the Shire-gemot; they were permitted to sue and be sued in the courts of justice; their persons, their safety, their liberty, and their property were protected by express laws."—*Sharon Turner*, "*Hist. Ang. Sax.*," Vol. III., p. 59.

They were famous in Europe for their skill in gold embroidery. The mother of Alfred was his earliest and best teacher. His daughter inherited his genius and spirit, and was the 'wisest woman in England.' It might have been said of many a Saxon woman, in reference to the and freedom was general. Kingship had been born of battle; but the kings were little more than elective war chiefs, and the national council could depose them. Assemblies of freemen consulted and decided on public questions. County courts, which we have inherited, took cognizance of all cases, whether temporal or spiritual. Slavery was limited in extent, and the body of the people were proprietors or free laborers. Those of lower ranks could rise to the higher, like the great Earl Godwin. Towns and parishes were more numerous than on the Continent. Allodial properties were widely distributed; and the Witanagemote, or Assembly of Wise Men, including king, clergy, nobles, and gentry, held the government of the kingdom in its strong and liberal hand.

In spite, therefore, of wide illiteracy, and of unrefined manners, the Saxon people, at the time when Edward the Confessor completed his work of fifteen years in building Westminster Abbey, were comparatively self-governed, energetic, and prosperous. They had liberty of access, laymen as well as priests, to copies of the Scriptures, where these existed. The Gospel and the Epistle were read in English in the churches, and the sermon was so preached.* Other parts of the Scriptures were in their own tongue.

---

sturdy stock from which she sprang, as it was said of Edith, daughter of Godwin, who was singularly lovely in person and character, and of many accomplishments, "Sicut spina rosam, genuit Godwinus Editham."

* Lingard, "Hist. of Eng.," Vol. I., p. 307.

Ælfric, in the tenth century, had given an epitome of the Old and New Testaments, and had translated portions of them, besides quoting in his homilies numerous texts. The "Rushworth Gloss," like the Durham, gave the Latin of the gospels, with a Saxon translation; and still another translation of the same sacred records is known to have preceded the Conquest. It seems nearly certain that if the progress thus commenced had continued unhindered, long before the day of Wycliffe, the Bible, in the speech of the people, would have been the possession and rich inheritance of our rough, but robust, aspiring, and hopeful English ancestors.

At this point, however, breaks in upon their history a fracturing force, which certainly long retarded this progress, and which seemed for a time wholly to forbid the final attainment. I refer, of course, to the Norman Conquest.

The difference between the Saxon and the Norman was not one of blood, since both represented the Teutonic stock; but it was fuller of meaning and of menace for that very reason, because the Scandinavian stuff had taken in the Normans a peculiar development, which made them at once despise and hate their ancient kinsman. Their long career as rovers of the seas had perfected in them the native fierceness from which the Saxons had been emerging into a more domestic habit. Settling in France, in the ninth century, and wresting lands and cities from its king, these restless pirates—whom Charlemagne, even at the height of his power, had seen and feared—entered into alliance with the Southern civilization, and became its chiefest Northern champions. Dropping their own religion and language, they adopted the religion, the language, and the manners, which preceded them in France. Its feudal system, in the utmost completeness, they joyfully accepted. Its rites of chivalry, which the Saxons had tardily and partially adopted, were practised by them with eager devotion, as well as with prodigal splendor and pomp. They became the exulting, if not always the patient, adherents of the Papacy, whose far-ascending orders of rank surpassed their elaborate feudal distinctions, whose majestic ceremonial was more sumptuous and brilliant than that of their tournaments. And a century and a half after their first settlement in France, there was no province, from the Channel to the Gulf, more alive than was theirs with the spirit and forms of the peoples speaking the Romance tongues. The martial fire burned as ever in their veins; but their constitution was feudal, their language French, the whole tone of their society had been caught from the South.

Descendants of renowned and irresistible conquerors, "the silver streak" interposed but slight barrier between this people and the fertile farms and thriving towns every rumor of which reëxcited their greed. Their influence had been largely augmented in England during the reign of Edward the Confessor. It came to its terrific consummation when on Christmas-day, A.D. 1066, a few weeks after the victory of Hastings, William of Normandy was crowned King of England, in that Westminster Abbey whose vast extent, massive pillars, and cruciform structure showed already the Norman impress. His conquest was not fully completed till some years after; but from that time the old order of things was practically ended, and a new and dreadful era began.

The destruction of properties in the kingdom was enormous. The destruction of life, happiness, hope, not only in battle, but in the fierce outrage and rapine which broke as a fiery flood upon the land, is something which cannot be pictured in speech. It is not wonderful that men fancied long afterward that fresh traces of blood appeared supernaturally on the battle-ground near Hastings, as if to show the writhing of the land in its immense anguish. In the time of Stephen, the Chronicle said, one might travel a day and not find one man living in a town, nor any land under cultivation. "Men said openly that Christ and his Saints were asleep."* The

---

* See Hallam, "Mid. Ages," Vol. II., p. 316.

"Between York and Durham every town stood uninhabited; their streets became lurking-places for robbers and wild beasts. . . . . Men, women, and children died of hunger; they laid them down and died in the roads and in the fields, and there was no man to bury them. . . . . Nay, there were those who did not shrink from keeping themselves

feudal system, in all its rigor, took the place of the simpler Saxon institutions; and it was reckoned, in the third generation after the Conquest, that more than eleven hundred castles had already been erected. The Saxon clergy, endeared to the people by their general steadfastness for the popular cause, were driven with violence from their places, to be succeeded by Norman monks. Wulfstan, of Worcester, was, after a little, the only Bishop of English blood left in his place. The supremacy of the Pontiff, who had sent to William his consecrated standard, and who had followed his invasion with the first Papal legates in the island, appeared finally exalted above all local Episcopal rights; and the freedom of the Church seemed to have fallen, with that of the State, in final ruin. Even venerated Saxon saints were displaced from the calendar, as if Heaven itself were a wholly Norman institution.

The language of the people was banished from the Court, the councils, the public records, and the Northern dialect of France took its place. The native

---

alive on the flesh of their own kind."—*Freeman, Hist. Nor. Conq.*, Vol. IV., p. 293.

"England was now a scene of general desolation, a prey to the ravages both of natives and foreigners. Fire, robbery, and daily slaughter, did their worst on the wretched people, who were forever attacked, trampled down, and crushed. . . . . Ignorant upstarts, driven almost mad by their sudden elevation, wondered how they arrived at such a pitch of power, and thought that they might do whatever they liked."—*Orderic Vital. Eccl. Hist.*, B. IV., chs. iv., viii.

English were despised without measure, and despoiled without mercy. Many fled across the sea, into the service of foreign kings, or of the Greek Emperor. Becket — made Chancellor, and Archbishop, under Henry Second — was the first Englishman to rise to any distinguished office;* and during the intervening century it seemed as if the earlier nation had been literally crushed, by the fierce onset of overwhelming power, into a helpless and hopeless subjection, from which there could be no release.

It could not but be long, under circumstances like these, before the tendencies, active before, had a chance to reappear, seeking again a freer faith, and wider acquaintance with the Scriptures. But these tendencies, like those to freedom in the State, were radical and perennial; and the stubborn struggle through which they at last rose to supremacy makes the pages which record it of interest to the world.

In spite of this tremendous overthrow, which had fallen like a whirlwind full of thunder and flame on the English people, and in spite of the organized military oppression under which they long suffered, many things remained, and after a time reässerted their right. The old language remained; and gradually, though slowly, it crowded back the Norman dialect,

---

* It is extremely doubtful if Becket was of Saxon descent; (see Milman, Lat. Christ., Vol. IV., pp. 309-312); but that he was regarded by the English as their representative, in a sense in which none of his predecessors had been, is beyond question.

while from that it gained important additions. The old laws continued, among the people, and the early local institutions. These gradually attacked the fabricated strength of the feudal establishment; and every prince who would win popularity found his readiest resource in ratifying the laws of Edward the Confessor. The old life of the people remained, unbroken by the desolating strokes it had suffered, and with an unconquerable tenacity of purpose waiting its time to conquer its conquerors.

Meantime, it grew evident that many things had come with the Conquest, to expand, enrich, and liberalize this life, and to make the nation ultimately nobler, in knowledge and in hope. The monastic school of the Bec, in Normandy, was famous throughout Europe, and the great archbishops, Lanfranc[*] and Anselm, who came thence to Canterbury, established schools, quickened thought, and fostered learning. A more uniform church-service was established in the kingdom, making worship more attractive with its statelier harmonies.[†] Our very word "Bible," as de-

---

[*] "To understand the admirable genius and erudition of Lanfranc, one ought to be an Herodian in grammar, an Aristotle in dialectics, a Tully in rhetoric, an Augustine and a Jerome, and other expositors of law and grace, in the sacred Scriptures. Athens itself, in its most flourishing state, ... would have honoured Lanfranc in every branch of eloquence and discipline, and would have desired to receive instruction from his wise maxims."—*Orderic Vital., Eccl. Hist.*, B. IV., ch. vii.

[†] "Hereupon Osmund, Bishop of Salisbury, devised that ordinary, or form of service, which hereafter was observed in the whole realm.

scribing the Scriptures, came with the Normans into England. New learnings were absorbed from the now nearer Continent. The civil and the canon law became the subjects of careful study. Distinguished scholars acquired a European fame: John of Salisbury, with William of Malmesbury, in the twelfth century; Matthew Paris, the historian, and sharp critic of Rome, in the thirteenth, with Roger Bacon, greatest of mediæval philosophers, and Robert Grostête, Bishop of Lincoln, most distinguished of prelates;* Occam, the "invincible" and the "unique," in the fourteenth century, with Thomas Bradwardine, pro-

---

.... Henceforward the most ignorant parish-priest in England, having no more Latin in all his treasury, yet understood the meaning of *secundum usum Sarum*, that all service must be ordered 'according to the course and custom of Salisbury church.'"—*Fuller, Church Hist. of Brit.*, B. III., Sec. 1, § 23.

* Matthew Paris' description of him is worth quoting for its simplicity and force, and as incidentally illustrating the spirit of the time:

"Pendant sa vie, il avait réprimandé publiquement le seigneur pape et le roi, corrigé les prélats, réformé les moines, dirigé les prêtres, instruit les clercs, soutenu les écoliers, prêché devant le peuple, persécuté les incontinents, fouillé avec soin les divers écrits, et avait été le marteau et le contempteur des Romains. .... Il avait gagné le respect de tous par son zèle infatigable à remplir les fonctions pontificales.

"Lorsqu'il mourut, à savoir la nuit où il monta vers le Seigneur, Foulques, évêque de Londres, entendit au plus haut des airs un son très-doux, dont la mélodie pouvait à juste titre récréer et charmer les oreilles et le cœur de celui qui l'entendait. .... Alors l'évêque: Par le foi que je dois à Saint Paul, je crois que le vénérable évêque de Lincoln, notre père, notre frère, et notre maître, a passé de ce monde, et est déjà placé dans le royaume du ciel."—*Chron. de Mat. Par. trad. par Huillard-Bréholles*, Tome VII., p. 445.

found in mathematics as well as in theology. Churches and monasteries were built in great numbers: the cathedrals of Canterbury, Durham, Rochester, Chichester, Norwich, Winchester, Gloucester, and others The Norman spirit and manner of treatment gave from the first a new character to such buildings, which afterward flowered into delightful exhibition in the pointed arches or the lovely flowing window-tracery of later cathedrals, as Salisbury, or Wells, or in the Westminster chapel of St. Stephen.

The Universities were organized at Oxford and Cambridge, and attracted wide public attention.* An immense enthusiasm for study prevailed among the young. In the thirteenth century Oxford was second only to Paris in the number of its students. Thirty thousand are said to have been there at one time, to learn, as Hume says, "bad Latin, and worse logic," but to gain enlargement and vigor of thought from even such imperfect studies; and it was the logic of Aristotle which came there, through Edmund Rich, afterward Archbishop. The arts of music and pictorial illustration took a fresh impulse. The use of paper, instead of parchment, multiplied manuscripts.

---

* "Giraldus Cambrensis, about 1180, seems the first unequivocal witness to the resort of students to Oxford, as an established seat of instruction. But it is certain that Vacarius read there on the civil law in 1149, which affords a presumption that it was already assuming the character of a university."—*Hallam, Lit. Hist. Europe.*, Vol. I., p. 16.

The first charter of Oxford was granted by Henry III., A.D. 1244.

The first really English book, the travels of Sir John Mandeville, appeared in the middle of the fourteenth century; and libraries then began to be gathered by private persons. Better than all, the Norman and the Saxon elements, so long exasperated into mutual hate, began to assimilate, and to come into union, to form the ultimate English people; and so the old spirit, which had survived Bede and Alfred, and had outlived the Conquest, was ready again, with larger training, ampler instruments, a more complete strength, to take up its interrupted work.

Already, in the reign of Henry Second, the Norman had begun to cease to be conqueror, while the Saxon began to rise from subjection. He "initiated," it has been said, "the rule of Law." Early in the thirteenth century Magna Charta was won, by the people as well as by barons and clergy, in the interest of all; and distinctions of descent thenceforth in large measure disappeared. Under Henry Third was added the memorable Charter of the Forest, while the Great Charter was solemnly reäffirmed. How frequently afterward it was so reäffirmed, every one knows: by the weak king, needing popular support; by the strong king, wanting money for wars. Edward Third reäffirmed it fifteen or more times, in his single reign. Within two centuries after the Conquest, A.D. 1265, Parliament included citizens and burgesses, with nobles and prelates. Its name was Norman, its substance English. In the fourth year of Edward

Progress of the English Law.

Third it was ordained that its sessions should be annual; and it constantly insisted on conditions precedent before making its grants, these conditions being the enlarged and secured liberties of the realm. Under the Edwards immense progress was thus made in the law; and the Royal prerogative, in spite of the glamour cast upon it by the later French victories, sensibly declined.

The treatise of Glanville, the earliest probably on English law, had been written before; and that of Bracton had followed it, under Henry Third. The famous treatise known as "Fleta," of the reign of Edward First, composed probably by order of the king; the tract of Britton, in Norman French; the "Mirror of Justice," written perhaps a little later, and probably by a Saxon—these show the progressive activity in legal discussion. Year-books, containing authentic reports of adjudged cases, began in the reign of Edward Second. A great number of fruitful new laws came into existence under Edward Third, and on points of capital importance. The power of the people was more clearly recognized. They had shown their prowess on Continental fields, and the skilled archers, to whose English muscle the Norman arrow had given a swift and terrible weapon, had won the day for belted knights at Crécy and at Poictiers. Even the enfranchisement of the villain-class was steadily advancing; and the near insurrection, headed by Wat Tyler, only manifested in sudden and riotous fury the spirit which had long preceded and impelled it.

The English language, now enriched from the French, came again to its place, not among the people only, but at the Court. In A.D. 1258, two centuries after the Conquest, was first issued a Royal proclamation in English. The Chancellor's speech was made in Parliament in the same tongue, a century later, A.D. 1363. But, a year before, it had been ordered that pleas in Court should be pleaded and judged in English, though laws and records continued to be written in Latin or in French. This was at once a sign and a stimulant of the revived national spirit, which had come once more to animate the kingdom; and this had its ultimate menace toward the Pope, as well as toward immediate secular oppressions.

The exactions of the Papacy in the thirteenth century had been nearly intolerable, in spite of the fact that Magna Charta had interposed its shining shield to protect in a measure the national Church. The Norman work had been only too thoroughly done. The richest benefices were held by foreigners. One half of the real estate in the kingdom belonged to the Church. Vast sums were annually sent from it, to pass out of sight through the lavish treasury of Rome or Avignon. The finances of the Crown were embarrassed thereby, while the popular indignation grew vehement and wide. The removal of the Papal throne into France, early in the century, had shaken the English allegiance to it. The long Schism of the West, which closed the century, in which England and France favored rival pontifical claimants, struck a heavier blow at the popular regard for the office itself. The drift of English legislation became therefore sharply and stubbornly adverse at least to the secular claims of the Pope.

In the seventh year of Edward First, the statute of Mortmain limited the acquisition of properties by the Church. In the eighteenth year of Edward Third, this was renewed and its execution more fully assured. In the twenty-fifth year of the same signal reign the statute of "Provisors" forbade Papal encroachment on the rights of those who should present to church-offices; and two years after, this was brought to a cutting edge by the sharp writ of "Praemunire"— a barbarous name for a righteous procedure—which was further defined and reinforced in the sixteenth year of Richard Second, by what the Pope not unnaturally called "an execrable statute":* which put out of the king's protection any who should procure at Rome translations, processes, excommunications, bulls, or other instruments, against the king and his dignity, forfeiting their goods, attaching their persons, and subjecting them to imprisonment at the king's

---

* "Quamvis dudum in regno Angliæ jurisdictio Romanæ ecclesiæ, et libertas ecclesiastica fuerit oppressa, vigore illius execrabilis statuti etc."—*Letter of Martin Fifth, to the Duke of Bedford.*

pleasure. It was the flash of a naked blade, warning the Pope to keep his hands off from England; and this same writ of "Praemunire" became a weapon of terrible effect, two centuries after, in the furious grasp of Henry Eighth.*

It is apparent, then, that we at last have reached a point where many conditions were favorable in England to the revival of the earlier movement toward freedom in religion, and toward unhindered popular acquaintance with the books of the Scripture. Yet it must not fail also to be noticed that two forces were moving, distinctly, and with violence, in the opposite direction, which were in fact only deepened and made swifter by the general obvious progress toward freedom. The one was the jealous, excited, passionate spirit of leading prelates, like Wykeham or Courtenay, whose power was still subtle and immense, and who were more strenuous for the spiritual place and prerogative of the Church, as they felt the State crowding upon their secular establishment. The other—in some respects the more dangerous force—was the jealousy of land-owners, as the peasants around them were seen to be rising toward larger liberties.

---

* A very ample and clear analysis of the famous statutes of "Provisors" and "Praemunire" is given in Reeves' "History of the English Law," Vol. II., pp. 259-269.

Fuller's comment is, as usual, quaint and vigorous: "Some former laws had pared the Pope's nails to the quick; but this cut off his fingers in effect, so that hereafter his hands could not grasp and hold such vast sums of money as before."—*Church Hist. of Brit.*, B. IV., Sec. 1, §33.

The repeated breaking out of the plague in England, with its terrible ravages—cutting off, it is supposed, nearly half the population—had unsettled all conditions of labor, and men were lacking to do necessary work, while harvests rotted on the ground, and cattle wandered at their will. Successive statutes, beginning in A.D. 1349, had sought to compel the service of laborers, and to regulate prices; but they constantly failed, for forty years, and the fear and wrath of proprietors were aroused against the turbulence re-excited and extended by these very laws. Any influence which promised additional impulse to the peasant-class must therefore encounter their fierce resistance; while, as I have said, the prelates, bred in the traditions of Rome, were only more watchful against every threatened moral assault because they had to yield and bend to the will of Parliament concerning the enlargement of their temporal estates.

This was substantially the state of England in the middle of the fourteenth century; and it is in the midst of this excited, fermenting life—on the front of this old, yet ever-new movement, toward freedom, nationality, and a more intelligent popular faith—between these sharply threatening perils—that the figure of John Wycliffe confronts us. It is obvious, I think, that he appeared at a critical time; that many forces had contributed to determine his spirit and aims, and to assign him his work in the world; and that that work, although it came in the fulness of time, was one of the most difficult, as well as of the largest, yet entrusted to any man. I think it will appear, too, that he was of singular fitness for it, and did it with a supreme fidelity; and that the fruit of it never has passed from English history. In some respects, certainly, his is one of the most impressive of all the figures which his time presents. The Saxon and the Norman were singularly combined in the great Englishman, at once scholar and statesman, philosopher and ambassador, devout recluse and determined reformer. And we, to-night, may well be conscious of real and rich indebtedness to him.

The principal outward incidents of his life are sufficiently familiar. He was born in Yorkshire, not far from Richmond, famous for its noble castle, on an estate which had belonged to his family from the time of the Conquest. The earlier elements of the English population had continued in that district in larger numbers, and had clung to the old traditions of the kingdom with greater tenacity, than in the midland and southern counties,* though Wycliffe's own family, to the end of its history, remained attached with peculiar zeal to the Roman Church. It

---

* "The Norman successors of the Bastard dwelt in full safety in the Southern provinces, but it was scarcely without apprehension that they journeyed beyond the Humber; and a historian of the twelfth century [William of Malmesbury] tells us that they never visited that part of their kingdom without an army of veteran soldiers. It was in the North that the tendency to rebel against the social order established by the Conquest longest endured."—*Thierry*, "*Nor. Conq.*," Vol. I., p. 294.

seems, indeed, to have carefully covered the natural traces of his inheritance in it, to whose fame alone it owes remembrance.

In the year 1324, according to the common statement, or, more probably, a little earlier, the boy John was here born. Of his instruction in childhood, we have no special knowledge, as indeed he has told us almost nothing of his life, at any point, being too great for egotism, and too much engrossed with public work to perpetuate the incidents of his personal history; but probably about the year 1335, he went to Oxford, and entered one of the five colleges then there existing—either Merton or, as seems more probable, Balliol, with which he was certainly afterward connected, and which had been founded by a family whose estates lay near his home. He was at the University a "Borealis," or member of the northern "Nation," which had its own Proctor, and which represented whatever was freest in the spirit of the place; and the whole University—which was then simply a vast public school—constituted a democratic cosmopolitan society, in which knowledge gave leadership, and in which the scholars of different countries were equally at home. Richard of Armagh, not yet Archbishop, was in Oxford at the time, of whom Neander speaks as "a forerunner of Wycliffe, by his freedom of thought;"[*]

---

[*] Hist. of Church, Vol. V., p. 134.

and Thomas Bradwardine had recently been there, who anticipated Edwards in his doctrine of the will, and whose vigor of character made all his speculation energetic and impressive. How far the young student was in contact with such teachers cannot be affirmed; but doubtless the fine and fervid spirit which emanated from them affected all minds as responsive as his, and all hearts as deeply touched with a sense of religion.

He became, of course, familiar with Latin, as then used among scholars, but not with Greek, which was not yet at home in Oxford; and the liberal arts, grammar, rhetoric, and logic — the "Trivium,"— arithmetic, astronomy, geometry, and music — the "Quadrivium,"—we know that he successfully pursued. The physical and mathematical studies, indeed, appear to have had for him quite as strong an attraction as the logical and speculative. He passed from them all to the study of Theology, including the interpretation of the Old and New Testaments, as found in the Vulgate, the reading of the Fathers, and of the Scholastic Doctors, with the study of the canon law. That he studied also the civil law, then or afterward, is equally certain, with the history and the canonical law of his own kingdom. And these were to bear large fruit in his life.

In such pursuits probably ten years were occupied, and by A.D. 1345, or thereabouts—the year before Crécy, four years after Petrarch had been crowned at the Capitol—he was fitted for larger University-work, as a teacher and a Master. It is not necessary to follow his course for the twenty years afterward, which were years with him of silent growth, in preparation for a service which he could then have scarcely expected. After A.D. 1357 he was for some time a Fellow of Merton College; in A.D. 1361 he was Master of Balliol; and the same year he was nominated by his college Rector of Fylingham, a Lincolnshire parish, which allowed him to continue in connection with Oxford. For a short time he was Warden of Canterbury Hall, appointed by the Archbishop, its founder, on account of his excellencies of learning and of life,* but soon removed by the successor of the prelate; and in A.D. 1366 he first appeared upon the stage of national affairs, and began to gather that broader brightness about his name which was finally to become a shining and enduring splendor. To understand his attitude and course, at that time and after, we must recall their particular and controlling public conditions.

In the year before, 1365, Urban Fifth had made claim upon Edward for the payment of a thousand marks, as the annual feudal tribute promised by John

---

* "Ad vitæ tuæ et conversationis laudabilis honestatem, literarumque scientiam, quibus personam tuam in artibus magistratum altissimus insignivit, mentis nostræ oculos dirigentes, ac de tuis fidelitate, circumspectione, et industria plurimum confidentes," etc.—*Quoted by Vaughan*, "*Life of Wycliffe*," Vol. I., p. 417.

to Innocent Third for the kingship of England, and also for payment of large arrears due on such tribute. Edward, in whose reign it had never been paid, referred this to Parliament; and that body was assembled in the following May. Its prompt and emphatic decision was, that such a tribute should not be paid; that John had had no right to pledge it, and had violated his oath of Coronation in the act; and that, if the Pope should prosecute the claim, the whole power of the kingdom should be set to resist him. This defiant decision was sufficient for its purpose, and the claim was never again presented. From that time on, England stood free from any pretence to vassalage toward the Pope, and had its path more clear than before to future freedoms.

It is probable that Wycliffe was a member of this Parliament, representing the clergy, or summoned by the king.* He was, at all events, so prominent an advocate of its decision, that a champion of the Papacy made upon him a vehement assault, in reply to which he gives the reasons urged in Parliament, by temporal lords, against such a tribute. From these he concludes that the treaty of John had been invalid and immoral; and he so presents the reasons

---

* The facts which make this probable are clearly and largely stated by Lechler ["John Wiclif," etc., Vol. I., pp. 200-214], and the subsequent increasing influence of the Reformer, with the Court, and in the country, seems naturally to start from such an early position of special public trust and prominence.

for this as to show his profound sympathy with them, if he had not himself suggested and shaped them. He calls himself, at the outset of his tract, "an obedient son of the Church of Rome;" and such, no doubt, he then felt himself to be. But the vivid spirit of nationality and of liberty which appears in the tract, with the habit of referring to permanent equities as properly controlling in public affairs, was prophetic of much; and the instinct of the Papacy must already have felt in him its future effective and intrepid assailant. He was, at this time, you observe, perhaps forty-five years of age, a distinguished scholar, according to the best standard of the time, famous as a philosopher, an influential churchman, prominently connected with the leading University. Now that his spirit was clearly declared, equally fearless, searching, and sagacious, now that the expert and practised logician had shown himself also skilled in affairs, it might justly be expected that his work would widen, and his influence become a large and beneficent national force.

Academical and royal distinctions soon came to him, as he was made Doctor in the faculty of Theology, and, perhaps, royal chaplain; and in A. D. 1374 he was appointed by the king a member of the commission sent to treat with a Papal embassy, at the city of Bruges, on matters of grave and long dispute. His name stands second on this commission, following that of the Bishop of Bangor; and the members were empowered to conclude a just compact on the matters in question with the Papal nuncios. The commission was associated with a large and brilliant civil embassy, at the head of which was the Prince's brother, the Duke of Lancaster, with the Earl of Salisbury, and the Bishop of London.

Then, probably for the first time, Wycliffe saw a foreign city, and one which presented as striking a contrast to anything in England as did perhaps any town on the Continent. The busy, wealthy, populous Bruges was then at the height of its middle-age fame: with the picturesque building just erected, whose belfry-chimes still ring in the square, and are echoed in poetry, with twenty ministers of foreign kingdoms having hotels within the walls, and with companies of merchants there established from all parts of Europe; while, at the time of Wycliffe's visit, were gathered there also royal princes and nobles of France, with prelates from Italy, Germany, and Spain. Wycliffe was brought there into closer relations with John of Gaunt, Duke of Lancaster, whose friendship was afterward important to him; and it well may be that a fresh impression of the lovely and austere majesty of the Gospel, and of the simplicity of that earlier development of Christianity in the world with which his studies had made him familiar, came upon his spirit, while he saw, as in microcosmic view, the ostentation and pride, the practical unbelief, and the hardly veiled license, which were the abounding fruit in Europe of undisputed Pontifical rule. One cannot but think that many convictions, which were governing with him in subsequent life, took emphasis if not origin from his brief residence in the gay and luxurious Flemish town.

The general result of the labors of the commission was not of importance. Some of its members were soon promoted by the Pope, and it is not perhaps a violent inference that they had been acting from the first in his interest. Wycliffe certainly was not promoted, save as he was lifted to fresh prominence and influence by the sharp prelatical attacks made upon him; and this may warrant us in presuming that he had been faithful to king and realm, in the exciting scenes and service. In A.D. 1374 he was made by the king Rector of Lutterworth, with which his name was ever after to be connected; and, as I have said, the steadfast stuff of which he was made, his ability, energy, and loyalty to freedom, were soon further tested in public affairs.

In A.D. 1376 the Parliament, afterward known as "the good Parliament," was assembled, before which came the complaints of the kingdom against the Papacy, and by which these complaints were presented to the king. The continued intrusion of foreign clergy into English church-livings, the scandalous character of many who bought these from Papal brokers, the decay of religion consequent upon it, with the pecuniary exhaustion of the kingdom by the sums drained from it to be spent in dissolute pleasures abroad—these were some of the vehement complaints; and the fact that in England was a Papal collector, gathering tribute to be sent to the Pope, and claiming the first-fruits of church-livings, was specially presented, with sharp remonstrance. It is probable that Wycliffe was a member of this Parliament, and that its complaints were shaped by his hand. The very language in which they are framed seems marked with his idiom, and the relation suggested between moral disorder and the physical calamities which troubled the realm, is exactly in his spirit.

In the following year, 1377, he attacked Garnier, the Papal collector, with indignant intensity, and, passing beyond the subordinate agents, with profound moral earnestness he challenged the system which made them possible. He came thus at last into that personal grapple with the Pontiff which might from the first have been foreseen: maintaining that he can sin; that what he does is by no means right because he does it; that he is bound to be preëminent in following Christ, in humility, meekness, and brotherly love; implying, plainly, that otherwise he is no Pope at all. The crowning doctrine here appears that Holy Scripture is for the Christian the rule and standard of the truth, and that what conflicts with it has no authority. He is steadily advancing on the path of the principles to which study, reflection, public service have brought him, without looking back.

He has won, already, a high place in England, and he uses his power for freedom and truth with an unreserved outlay of strength which recalls the Saxon times and blood. It will evidently not do to leave him alone. At this point, therefore, breaks upon him the first onset of that Papal assault which was never afterward to cease to pursue him till his books had been prohibited, and his bones had been burned.

In February, A.D. 1377, he was summoned to appear before the Convocation, obviously on account of the stand which he had taken against prelatical and Papal aggression. When the Convocation assembled at St. Paul's, the Duke of Lancaster, and Percy, the Grand Marshal of England, with armed retainers, appeared with him, as friends and defenders; together with several personal friends, and some theologians who had come as his advocates. An altercation instantly arose, between the Marshal, with the Duke, on the one hand, and the imperious Bishop of London; the result of which was that Wycliffe was withdrawn from the tribunal without having had occasion to open his lips. Whatever purpose had been cherished against him, for the time at least had utterly failed, and he went out as free as before. Immediately, however, the English Bishops, or some of them, collected propositions affirmed to be his, forwarded them to Rome, and sought the Papal interposition. Of the nineteen propositions so presented, five referred to legal matters, as the rights of property and inheritance;

four concerned the right of rulers to withdraw from the Church its temporal endowments, if these should be abused; nine related to the power of Church discipline, with its necessary limits; and the closing one maintained that the Pontiff himself, being in error, may be challenged by laymen, and overruled. The "power of the keys," according to this clear-sighted witness, is only effective when used under the law of the Gospel; and no man can really be excommunicated unless by himself—unless, that is, he has given for it sufficient occasion.

On the basis of these articles Gregory Eleventh, in May, A.D. 1377, issued five bulls against their author. Three of them were addressed to the Archbishop, with the Bishop of London, commanding them to ascertain if such propositions had been in fact affirmed by Wycliffe, in "a detestable insanity," and if so, to imprison him until further instructions; commanding them also to cite him publicly, lest he should seek to escape by flight; and requiring them to bring the obnoxious articles to the notice of the king. Another bull was addressed to the king, informing him of the commission, and requiring his aid; and still another to the Chancellor and University of Oxford, enjoining them, on pain of loss of all their privileges, to commit Wycliffe and his disciples to custody, and deliver them to the authorized commission.

The death of Edward Third, with the accession of

Richard Second, which presently occurred, and the spirit opposed to the Papal court which appeared vividly in the following Parliament, made it expedient to delay taking action under these instruments; and it was not until the end of the year, after Parliament was prorogued, that proceedings commenced. Meantime, Wycliffe had drawn up an opinion, for the king and council, on the right of the kingdom to restrain its treasure from being carried to foreign parts, in defiance of Papal censure. With utmost emphasis he, of course, affirms this right: on the several grounds of the law of nature, the law of the Gospel, the law of conscience; and it is not likely that this opinion rendered any less fierce the hostility to him which was already intense at Rome.

A week before Christmas, the bull addressed to the University was sent to the Chancellor, with the demand that he ascertain if Wycliffe had propounded the alleged theses, and if so, to cite him to appear in London before the commission. The marked difference between this mandate and the sharper terms of the Papal bull shows a doubt of the temper which might prevail in the University, with a fear of probable popular sympathy with the accused. The heads of the University seem to have taken no action whatever on the Papal bull, but to have so far responded to the commission as to serve upon Wycliffe the required citation. Early, therefore, in A.D. 1378, the vigorous and undaunted theologian appeared before the Archbishop and Bishop, and made written answer for the theses. But he did not come in his own strength alone. He was now recognized as the faithful representative of a wide English feeling. The widow of the Black Prince, now Queen-Mother, sent an officer to the commission, charging the prelates to pronounce on him no sentence. The people of London forced their way into Lambeth Chapel, and showed their purpose to defend him. The result of the proceeding bore, therefore, no proportion to its threatening commencement; for, though he was forbidden to teach the specified theses—on the ground that they would give offence to the laity—he left the court, for the open air of streets and fields, with his freedom unfettered, with his prominence and power only increased, by the futile assault. The successive attacks of those who hated him had given him a distinction which he never seems to have sought for himself.

At just this time began that long Western Schism, in which Urban Sixth was acknowledged by England, Clement Seventh by France; in which, subsequently, there were three Popes at once, almost equally detestable, with equal violence anathematizing each other; and which was not closed till thirty years after Wycliffe's death. An immense impression was made upon him by this event; and from that time, not ceasing to be a diligent scholar, a patriotic counsellor, a devout theologian, he more and more came to the front as a radical and devoted Church reformer. The thin, tall figure, the sharply-cut features, the penetrating eye, the firm-set lips and flowing beard, which his portraits present, the thoughtful, earnest, dignified presence, of which all men took note, were thenceforth to be found in the perilous van of the long English battle for a liberated Church and a Scriptural faith.

In this supreme period of his life, a marked and even a rapid progress is to be observed in his judgments of truth, leading him toward, if not wholly to, the ultimate ground of the Protestant Reformation. The Lutheran doctrine of Justification by faith alone, he never reached;* but his mind detached itself rapidly and surely from many entangling previous opinions; it sought for truth on every side, with eager care and fruitful fervor; and as fast as he reached any certain conclusion he flung the most strenuous energy of his soul into the work of conveying it to others. His time was short; his work was noble and prolific.

A skilful, acute, and practised logician, a realist in

---

* "Turning now to the other side of faith, Wiclif evidently assumes that the kernel of faith is a state of *feeling*, a moral activity, when, in accord with the theology of his age, and agreeably to Aristotelian metaphysics, he lays particular stress upon the *fides formata*, and defines faith to be a steadfast cleaving to God or to Christ in love (*per amorem caritatis perpetuo adhærere*). . . . . For this reason, we can hardly expect beforehand to find Wiclif doing homage to the Pauline Reformation-truth of the justification of the sinner by faith alone."—*Lechler*, "*John Wiclif*," etc., Vol. II., p. 79.

philosophy, yet a theologian largely made by the heart, he took Reason and Authority as the sources of all religious knowledge: "Reason" representing the intuitive and instructed mind and conscience; "Authority" representing the Divine Scripture. To the claim of the latter on human submission he admits no limit. It is superior to all traditions and decrees; the fundamental charter and law of the Church. It is a book for every man; to be interpreted by the Christian for himself, with prayerfulness and humility, with a reasonable regard for the general Christian judgment of its contents, and especially for that of the great Church-Fathers, but with an implicit personal reliance on the present aid of the Holy Ghost to make evident its meaning, as Christ had opened it to His disciples. He was himself a profound and constant student of the Scriptures, quoting from them freely, showing comparison of part with part, and so saturating his mind with even their language that the Biblical phrase clings to his pen when it is set in freest motion. He sought always the spiritual sense, yet for that very reason was attentive to minute particulars of expression, and to the thought suggested by these in the highest moods of feeling. He found the very life of his spirit in the Word, and more and more, to the end of his career, engaged his soul in the study and the love of what he declares the most true, faultless, perfect, and holy Law of God.

In the doctrine derived by him from the Scriptures

he was substantially Augustinian, though of unfettered thought, and differing at some points from the illustrious Numidian. The Law of God is to him the basis and the measure of all dominion, in the State and in the Church; and in Redemption is the key to Creation. Salvation is of grace alone, not merited by good works, and the Lord Jesus Christ is its only Mediator. He is Divine in nature and work, yet also the centre and head of Humanity, set forth as such with manifold fulness; and the dignity of man's nature, with the realness and the reach of his moral responsibility, appears from the fact that a Being so august has intervened to redeem him.* Of the Virgin Mary the utmost which he affirms, in later years, is that she was probably sinless, but that it is folly to contend on the question, since belief in her sinlessness is nowise essential to salvation. Toward homage to images, and prayers to the Saints, he became pronounced in his antagonism, discerning the danger of idolatry to the image, and holding any devotion to a Saint only of value as it may nourish piety to the Lord. He did not indiscriminately recognize Saints —denying vehemently the power of the Church to canonize many concerning whose holiness she could

---

* "It was the worth of human nature, as arising from these facts [that God had made man in His likeness, and that Christ had died to save him 'unto the bliss of Heaven'] which rendered Wycliffe so much the foe of war, and so much devoted to the religious welfare of men."— Vaughan, "*Life of Wycliffe*," Vol. I., p. 328.

not have been certain. He held the doctrine of the Church Invisible—the body of the Elect—in which the impure can have no place, however distinguished in prelatical rank, they belonging to the "Church of the Malignants"; and in this true Church the priesthood is common to believers, and every priest set apart to the office has right to administer all the sacraments. The celibacy of the clergy—though it was his own rule—he indignantly denounced, when imposed upon others, as "unscriptural, hypocritical, and morally pernicious"; and if, as he conceives to be possible, all church-officials should give themselves to evil ways, the laity would compose the Church, and must displace and judge their rulers.

Of only two sacraments does he treat, Baptism and the Supper; and against the doctrine of transubstantiation he flung his whole force, in reverberating assault. Till A.D. 1378 he had received it as traditionally taught. An interval of questioning evidently followed. With all his power, in utmost energy of speech and spirit, after A.D. 1381 he repels and denounces it: as contrary to God's Word; contrary to the early tradition of the Church; as pregnant with all evil effects; the most dangerous of heresies ever "smuggled into the Church by cunning hypocrites."* He held in substance, from that time, the Lutheran doctrine of the eucharist: no local cor-

---

* *Lechler*, "*John Wiclif*," etc., Vol. II., pp. 177–184.

poreal presence of Christ in the consecrated wafer, but a spiritual presence, to be spiritually discerned. Yet, though the glorified body is in heaven, and is not re-created by any priest, or bruised by the teeth of any recipient,* there is a certain energy from it in the elements, as there is a certain presence of the soul in all parts of the body; and the believing communicant is the one for whom this has its efficacy. He finds no warrant for any sacrament except in express words of the Scripture; and the preaching of that is to him a true sacrament.

Very briefly, and of course imperfectly stated, this is substantially the doctrinal system held by Wycliffe, in his mature and final thought; and when we recall his resolute spirit, his fervent zeal, and sovereign courage, with his deep sense of the calamities of the time, and his hope for the final reformation of Christendom, we easily see how inevitably he stood, by reason of it, toward the Papacy, as an enemy, definite and unsparing; toward the Scriptures, as counting no labor too great, and no sacrifice too costly, for their widest distribution.

In his relation to the Papacy three stages are apparent. Till A.D. 1378 he had recognized the primacy of the Bishop of Rome, while holding him

---

* As Raymond Lull expressed it: "Fuit unquam ullum mirabile vel ulla humilitas, quæ cum ipso possit comparari, ... quod tuum corpus adeo nobile se permittat *manducari et tractari* ab homine peccatore misero"?—See *Neander*, "*Hist. Church*," Vol. IV., p. 336 (note).

by no means infallible, or possessed of plenary spiritual power, and sharply rejecting his right to intermeddle with State legislation. From that time till A.D. 1381 he less and less esteemed the Papacy, as having any Divine authority, and came to think it desirable for the Church to dispense with both Popes, then clamoring for allegiance. And from A.D. 1381 to the day of his death, the Pope was to him the veritable antiChrist; the pontifical claims were flatly blasphemous; the Papal office had been a device of the Adversary of souls, and the homage paid to it was detestable idolatry. No words of the Reformers of the sixteenth century were ever more sweeping in severity toward the Papacy than were the words of this churchman of England, this eminent leader in its foremost University, five hundred years since; and all men might be sure that if ever a Pope should get opportunity, the sword or the flame would have one swift victim!

In connection with this assault on the Papacy he came to conflict with the Mendicant Orders, to attack whom at that time was to make the kingdom bristle with enemies. He had had with them mainly pleasant relations till A.D. 1378, and had rather exempted them from the fiery censures which he even then visited on the secular clergy; but from that time, especially after A.D. 1381, as his opposition to transubstantiation became more vehement, and his temper toward the Pope took on its intensity, he opened a combat with these Orders which only grew in its unsparing energy till his death. The absolutism against which he revolted had in them its ubiquitous messengers; and he smote at them, as well as it, with sentences that cut like the blows of a blade. It was a combat from which they never fully recovered, and which their subsequent defenders and apologists have never forgiven.*

This was the necessary destructive side of his immense and incessant activity, after his work had fully opened. But the positive side, which gave to his efforts enduring and upbuilding power, was in the new teaching of Scriptural truth, and especially in that circulation of the Bible to which his whole character, all the aims of his life, and all his convictions, with a necessary force, inspired and impelled him. It is by this that he rises to real preëminence in his times; that he suddenly consummates, in a supreme action, the long preceding tendencies of history; that he hurled at the vast religious imperialism then dominating Europe the one weapon which it could not withstand; that he shot forth a force still felt in our age, and which will not cease to extend itself in the world till the history of that has reached its conclusion amid the ultimate prophesied brightness. It was his princi-

---

* The full discussion by Lechler of the date of Wycliffe's controversy with the Mendicant Orders—usually assigned to A.D. 1360—justifies his declaration that "there is no truth in the tradition that Wiclif, from the very first, was in conflict especially with the Mendicant Orders. . . . . But from the year 1381 . . . . he opened a conflict with the Mendicant Monks, which went on from that time till his death with ever-increasing violence."—"*John Wiclif*," etc., Vol. II., pp. 140-146.

pal earthly work; and it gives him his final and grand renown.

I have spoken already of his fine and large acquaintance with the Scriptures, and of his profound spiritual sense of their majestic and tender meaning. It was always observed of him as a preacher that his discourse was rooted in the Bible; that while others preached 'chronicles of the world, and stories from the battle of Troy,' he clung to the Scripture, and derived from that his illuminating lessons. "The highest service that man may attain to on earth," he says, "is to preach God's Word." "O, marvellous power of the Divine seed," he says again, "which overpowers the strong man armed, softens obdurate hearts, and changes into Divine men those who were brutalized in sin, and removed to an infinite distance from God." He insisted on simplicity, clearness, energy, in developing and applying the message of the Word; on devout feeling in the ministry of it, since, "if the soul be not in tune with the words, how can the words have power?" But ever it is the Word itself which is to him "the Life-seed, begetting regeneration and spiritual life;" and in all proclamation of the Gospel the aim must be so to flash its light on the spirit as to bend the will to its obedience.

Chaucer's picture of the good country priest, which has often been conceived to portray Wycliffe, represents him as diligent and benign, rich in holy thought and work, who has caught the words of life from the Gospel.* Whether or not the poet thought of this special preacher, he has aptly described him. He had seen the Lord; and the words which he had heard from Divine lips were law and life to his enthusiastic and resolute spirit. He would make them the power of God to others. So he sent forth his itinerant preachers, without shoes, in unbleached russet, to traverse the kingdom, and to make these words familiar in it. Probably these went out from Oxford as early as A.D. 1378—many of them with no clerical ordination, " Evangelical men," colporteurs we should say; with God's Law for their theme, their manner of preaching plain and simple, their contact

---

* " A good man was ther of religioun,
And was a pore Persoun of a town;
But riche he was of holy thought and werk.
He was also a lerned man; a clerk
That Cristes gospel gladly wolde preche;
His parischens devoutly wolde he teche.
Benigne he was, and wondur diligent,
And in adversite ful pacient.
* * * * *
" This noble ensample unto his scheep he yaf,
That ferst he wroughte, and after that he taughte,
Out of the gospel he tho wordes caughte.
* * * * *
" A bettre preest I trow ther nowher non is,
He waytud after no pompe ne reverence,
Ne maked him a spiced conscience,
But Cristes lore, and his apostles twelve,
He taught, and ferst he folwed it himselve."

Prol. to Cant. Tales, Ald. Ed., Vol. II., p. 16.

with the people constantly close. He who sent them was anticipating Wesley, in the means which he used to evangelize England. He was multiplying his voice a hundred-fold, and planting his convictions, with an instant success, in multitudes of minds.

But now, as the greatest of all instruments for this supreme work, he would have God's Word itself translated into the common tongue of the people, and reproduced in manifold copies, till the peasant might have it, while the rich should gain through it a rarer treasure than jewels of price. This was not a mere measure of policy, for promoting a cause. It was, the fruit of a Christian instinct, as deep in his soul as life itself. He had felt the inexpressible power of the Scripture, to uplift and expand, to cheer and inspire the human spirit. He had felt, as profoundly as had Bernard, the overwhelming sense of the awfulness of life in its relation to unseen eternities, and the supreme ministry of the Gospel to this. It was thus an impulse irresistible within him to make the message which had come from the Most High accessible to all, till precept and promise, prophecy and truth, should be to men a presence as familiar as the sunshine in which they had their physical image. So he gave to his country the first English Bible,* to

---

* Sir Thomas More claimed to have seen copies of an English Bible earlier than Wycliffe's. He doubtless mistook, for such, copies of Wycliffe's first translation, before the revision. No trace remains of any complete version earlier than that; and those who suffered on account of

be multiplied only in manuscript copies, to be read, perhaps, only by stealth, but to be thenceforth the possession of England, and to put an influence into its life, and into the life which has subsequently flowed from it, across either hemisphere, which cannot be outlined in any discourse, or measured in thought. It was not only the greatest work attempted in the age, and in its effect the most beneficent; it was one of the most fundamental and momentous done in the world since the day when Paul took up his illustrious mission to the Gentiles.

Of the parts of the Bible known to the Saxons, I have previously spoken. It needs only to be added that the "Ormulum," so called, a paraphrase in verse of the Gospels and Acts, had been made in the thirteenth century, which seems, however, to have been confined to a single copy; that in the fourteenth century two translations of the Psalms had been made, and that these were followed, after a time, by one of the Epistles of Paul. But up to A.D. 1360 the Psalter was the only book of the Bible rendered into the common speech; and copies of this were certainly very rare. Within the next quarter of a century there came into the English language the entire Bible; and it came, by the witness of both adversaries and friends, through the impulse and the

---

that never justified themselves for having it by appealing to the existence of one preceding it.—*See Ed. of Wycliffe's Bible*, by Forshall and Madden, Preface, p. xxi. (note).

labor of the great "Reformer before the Reformation." How far he himself translated its books is not wholly certain. That he did so largely, is undisputed. A Harmony of the Gospels, first translated, seems to have led the way to the rest. The Apocalypse, with its incessant attraction for spirits like his, in times like those, was probably among the first of the books to engage his hand. Others followed: most of the New Testament being rendered by himself, doubtless with partial aid from friends, the Old Testament, probably, in good part, by Nicholas Hereford, an intimate friend and co-laborer with him. Hereford, however, seems to have been suddenly arrested in the work, and the rest to have been done by another, probably by Wycliffe.

Of course, all the translation had to be made from the Latin of Jerome, the Hebrew and Greek being almost unknown. It was, in other words, the version of a version, and so exposed to peculiar imperfection. But it must be remembered that Jerome had had early Greek manuscripts, earlier than any known until recently to the scholars of Europe, and that so in translating him Wycliffe stood at but one remove from the originals, while his perfect acquaintance with the Latin gave him ample opportunity to make his translation energetic and full as an English equivalent. He completed it probably as early, at the latest, as A.D. 1382; and copies of it were rapidly made, by the hands of skilled and eager scribes. But

Wycliffe himself no doubt was aware that the work had been too rapidly done for its highest value or best effect, and planned the revision, at once commenced, which finally appeared from the hand of John Purvey, in A.D. 1388, or four years after the master's death. Of this, more than a hundred and fifty manuscripts still remain, in whole or in part; many written on vellum, with elaborate care, to be the possession of churches, or of the wealthy, and not a few bearing the marks of long use, and of the concealment into which they were hurried in times of trouble.* All these were written, probably, within forty years after Wycliffe's death; and if we remember what destructive search for them was made in the day of persecution, how many went across the sea, how many shriveled in the fires of war, how many were burned, with those who had read them, in public squares, how many may yet wait to be discovered, we shall see how extraordinary their number at first must have been. Only a spirit intense and determined could have driven so swiftly so many pens.†

* In the "List of Manuscripts" prefixed by Forshall and Madden to their edition, one copy is described as "in an upright, large character, written with great care and neatness, about 1400": another, as having "initials to the books, in gold, upon coloured grounds, and to the chapters blue, flourished with red": another, with initials to the books "in colors and gold, branching into well-executed borders," etc.: one, as bound "in black silk, with silver clasps of the XVth century": another, "in green velvet, with brass bosses and clasps": one, as "much stained in parts": another, as having "suffered from damp": another, as "in parts much mutilated, torn, and soiled." pp. xxxix–lxiv.

† Westcott speaks of "about one hundred and seventy copies of the

Of the effect of this translation on the English language many have written. The judgment of Lechler is undoubtedly just, that "it marks an epoch in the development of the English language, almost as much as Luther's translation does in the history of the German tongues. The Luther Bible opens the period of the new High German. Wycliffe's Bible stands at the head of the Middle English."* The most recent historian of the English people speaks of him as the "Father of our later English prose."† Forms of expression still familiar in our version come directly from his: as the beam and the mote, the trampling of swine and the rending of dogs, the

---

whole, or part, of the Wycliffite versions which have been examined "— thirty, or more, of the first translation, the rest of Purvey's revision. He adds the interesting fact that "nearly half the copies are of a small size, such as could be made the constant daily companions of their owners." —"*Hist. Eng. Bible,*" p. 24.

* "*John Wiclif,*" etc., Vol. I., p. 347.

† "If Chaucer is the father of our later English poetry, Wyclif is the father of our later English prose. The rough, clear, homely English of his tracts, the speech of the ploughman and the trader of the day, though colored with the picturesque phraseology of the Bible, is, in its literary use, as distinctly a creation of his own as the style in which he embodied it, the terse vehement sentences, the stinging sarcasms, the hard antitheses which roused the dullest mind like a whip."— *Green's "Hist. of Eng. People,"* Vol. I., p. 489.

"The vocabulary of the reformers . . . . is drawn almost wholly from homely Anglo-Saxon, and the habitual language of religious life, while the lays of Gower and Chaucer are more freely decorated with the flowers of an exotic and artificial phraseology." *Marsh,* "*Lects. on Eng. Lang.,*" p. 168.

Comforter for the Paraclete, the Saxon exclamation "God forbid!" Mr. Marsh may state the matter too strongly when he calls the accomplished and diligent Tyndale "merely a full-grown Wycliffe"; adding that he "not only retains the general grammatical structure of the older version, but most of its felicitous verbal combinations, and, what is more remarkable, he preserves even the rhythmic flow of its periods."* It may be said in reply, as it has been, that much of what is common to the versions came into both out of the Vulgate, by which one was determined, the other influenced. Still it is true that what Mr. Marsh elsewhere calls "the sacred and religious dialect" which has continued the language of devotion and of Scriptural translation to the present day, was first established in England by the Wycliffe version;† and that what Mr. Froude has characterized as the peculiar genius, of mingled tenderness and majesty, of Saxon simplicity and preternatural grandeur, which breathes through the latest translation,‡ had its example, and partly its source, in the earliest. Tyndale, Coverdale, Rogers, Cranmer, the Geneva translators, King James' revisers, have all contributed something to the work, but they only heighten, without obscuring, its early lustre; and the final revision for which we look, with all the aids which the most untiring

---
* *Lects. on Eng. Lang.*, p. 627.
† *Lects. on Origin and Hist. Eng. Lang.*, p. 365.
‡ *Hist. of Eng.*, Vol. III., p. 86.

scholarship has gathered, must still abide, in its vocabulary, and in much of whatever charm it may possess through noble and harmonious forms of verbal combination, on the primitive foundations of five hundred years since.

How vast the impression produced by the version which thus burst into use, not on language only, but on life, in the whole sphere of moral, social, spiritual, even political experience, who shall declare! To the England of his time, confused, darkened, with dim outlook over this world or the next, the Lutterworth Rector brought the superlative educational force. He opened before it, in the Bible, long avenues of history. He made it familiar with the most enchanting and quickening sketches of personal character ever pencilled. He carried it to distant lands and peoples, further than crusaders had gone with Richard, further than Alfred's messengers had wandered. It saw again the "city of palms" in sudden ruin, and heard the echoes of cymbal and shawm from the earliest temple. The grandest poetry became its possession; the sovereign law, on which the blaze of Sinai shone, or which glowed with serener light of divinity from the Mount of Beatitudes. Inspired minds came out of the past—Moses, David, Isaiah, John, the man of Idumea, the man of Tarsus—to teach by this version the long-desiring English mind. It gave peasants the privilege of those who had heard Elijah's voice in the ivory palaces, of those who had seen the heaven opened by the river of Chebar, of those who had gathered before the "temples made with hands" which crowned the Acropolis. They looked into the faces of apostles and martyrs, of seers and kings, and walked with Abraham in the morning of time.

They stood face to face, amid these pages, with One higher than all; and the kingliest life ever lived on the earth became near and supreme to the souls which had known no temper in rank save that of disdain, no touch of power which did not oppress. Not only again, in lucid column, the pillar of fire marshalled God's hosts. Not only again were waters divided, and fountains made to gush from rocks. Angelic songs were heard once more, above the darkened earthly hills. Again, as aforetime, the Lord of Glory walked as a brother from Nazareth and from Bethany, strewing miracles in his path, yet leading the timid to the mount which burned with peaceful splendor, showing the penitent his cross, walking with mourners to the tomb. From the paradise of the past to the paradise above, the vast vision stretched; and gates of pearl were brightly opened above the near and murky skies. The thoughts of men were carried up on the thoughts of God, then first articulate to them. The lowly English roof was lifted, to take in heights beyond the stars. Creation, Providence, Redemption, appeared, harmonious with each other, and luminous with eternal wisdom; a light streamed forward on the history of the world, a brighter light on the vast and immortal experience of the soul; the bands of darkness broke apart, and the universe was effulgent with the lustre of Christ!

Of course this influence was not all felt by many minds; perhaps not in its fulness by any. But it was thenceforth at home in England; at home, to stay. It smote with irresistible energy on the rings and fetters of Pontifical rule. It contributed a force of expansion and uplift to every soul on which its quickening blessing fell. It became an instrument of popular liberty, as well as a means of elevation and grace to personal souls. There was the English Renaissance! Leighton, and Owen, and Jeremy Taylor, became possible afterward; Bacon and Hooker, Shakspeare and Milton, Dryden and Wordsworth, and Robert Burns. The world of letters had found a language for the majestic periods of Burke, for Addison's or Macaulay's prose, for Gibbon's sentences, moving as with the tread of an imperial triumph. The world of life had received to itself a transfiguring energy. Celestial forces mingled thenceforth, more vitally, widely, with human thought; and the indestructible holy influence, though often interrupted, never ceased, till it came to its final inevitable fruition in the perfect liberty of the Scriptures in England.*

---

* Hume speaks slightingly of Wycliffe—as might have been expected from a blind giant, discoursing of distant electric flames—but in no small measure he owed his opportunity to weave choice words into a

The subsequent months of Wycliffe's life were like the stormy afternoon, whose turbulence ceases, whose glooms are scattered, in the sunset's golden tranquillity. An ecclesiastical assembly at London—called by him "the Earthquake Council," because it was shaken by a tremble of the planet—condemned his doctrines, but left him untouched, apparently because of the spirit of the Commons.* Oxford repelled or evaded the attacks repeated upon him, but at last yielded to a royal mandate, and his long connection with it was closed. In November, A.D. 1382, he again defended his doctrine before the Provincial Synod assembled in Oxford, and again escaped personal sentence or assault. The weight of his character in the country was too great, his following was too large, to be challenged without danger. A vigorous memorial addressed to Parliament, against the English crusade for Urban, was one of his last public papers, though many brief tracts were written and distributed to the end of his life, and his sermons went forth as leaves on the wind. Three hundred of them still remain.

---

pleasing and perspicuous narrative to him of whom Dr. Vaughan has temperately said, that "his writings contributed, far more than those of any other man, to form and invigorate the dialect of his country."— *Life of Wycliffe*, Vol. I., p. 243.

* His characteristic comment on the assembly was: "The Council charged Christ and the Saints with a heresy; hence the earth trembled and shook, and a strong voice answered in the place of God, as it happened at the time of the last Passion of Christ, when He was condemned to bodily death."—*See Neander*, "*Hist. of Church*," Vol. V., p. 162.

He expected martyrdom,* and others as surely expected it for him. But he was of that iron temper which fire hardens into steel. His courage mounted with occasion; and he found it as true in his own time as it ever had been, "the nearer the sword, the nearer to God." In point of fact, he was never subjected to blade or brand. He wrought in patience at his Rectory, making it a centre of impulse to England. He stood to his convictions, whether the Pope cited him or not, though even the powerful John of Gaunt fell from his side, till a stroke of paralysis a second time smote him, as he was engaged in Divine offices, on the day of the Holy Innocents, at the close of the year 1384; and on the final day of that year, as reckoned by us, he passed out of earthly struggle and care, and entered his immortal rest.

LADIES AND GENTLEMEN:—I would not exaggerate anything in this man, but I am sure we must feel that it is with one of the heroical persons, making nations greater and histories splendid, that we have walked for a little this evening. Of course by his translation of the Scriptures he stands in most obvious relation to us. But the brightness of his fame in this connection may have concealed from the common thought the various and preëminent ability of the man, the large place which he filled in his time,

---

* "We have but to preach consistently [constanter] the law of Christ, even before the prelates of Cæsar, and a blooming martyrdom will promptly come, if we abide in faith and patience."—*Trialogus*, III, ch. 15.

the breadth and energy of his manifold influence. He does not loom into large proportions because we see him through morning mists. The more closely we study him, from different sides, the more surely will he win our admiring honor.

It is not often that a man without note, except among scholars, steps forward suddenly to a principal place in public counsel. He breaks into sight, amid the turmoil of his time, as a preordained leader, simply pushed to the front by an imperious impulse of nature. It is not often that a man addicted to subtle and large philosophical speculation proves practical and acute in the sphere of affairs. He was recognized as first among scholastic philosophers,* yet none surpassed him in political discussion, for force of statement, for grasp of principles, for sagacity or for daring. It is not often that one trained from childhood to familiar use of unclassical

---

* Henry Knighton, Canon of Leicester, and vehemently opposed to Wycliffe, yet spoke of him thus: "Doctor in Theologia eminentissimus in diebus illis. In philosophia nulli reputabatur secundus; in scholasticis disciplinis incomparabilis. Hic maxime nitebatur aliorum ingenia subtilitate scientiae et profunditate ingenii sui transcendere, et ab opinionibus eorum variare."—*See Vaughan's "Life of Wycliffe.,"* Vol. I., p. 247, (note).

Neander says of him: " In his pervading practical bent, we recognize a peculiarity of the English mind which has constantly been preserved. But to this was joined, in the case of Wiclif, an original speculative element; an element which, in those times, was also especially developed among the English, though at a later period it retired more into the background."—*Hist. of Church*, Vol. V., p. 135.

Latin becomes an attractive or a competent writer in a different tongue. He created an English style, rugged, idiomatic, whose sentences crash on the ear like grape-shot, whose words are half-battles, which has an occasional subtile charm, in the fine beauty of phrase and rhythm.

Blameless, reserved, ascetic in life,* he was humorous, too, with jests that were arguments, and with a severe, though a beneficent, sarcasm; as when it was said that the Scripture does not recognize friars; "but it does," was his answer, "in this text, 'I know you not'"! He was radical in his views, in Church and State, while a revered leader in a great University. Of knightly blood, and bred among students, till his alleged errors were attributed by his enemies to his subtlety of mind and inordinate learning, he judged the plain people more correctly than themselves; he interpreted the prophecy of their vague aspiration, and was not afraid of the final effect of even their wantonness. He had a deep sense of human sinfulness; but a nobler eulogy on human nature than ever was spoken was that wrought into action in his endeavor to make common to men the thoughts of God. The rector of a parish-church, he organized a mission which

---

* "His austere exemplary life has defied even calumny: his vigorous, incessant efforts to reduce the whole clergy to primitive poverty have provoked no retort as to his own pride, self-interest, indulgence, inconsistent with his earnest severity."—*Milman,* "*Lat. Christ.,*" Book xiii., ch. vi.

moulded the moral life of the kingdom, till every second man was a Lollard. In the solitude of his study, he dared to question the faith of ages, to plant himself on spiritual certainties, and to balance his mind, in the tranquillity of reason, against the whole shock of church-authority. Apparently neither seeking nor shrinking from contest, he smote the Pope with tremendous anathemas, at a time when heresy was more odious than treason, and when reverence for the Pontiff was the religion of Christendom. With instinctive prescience he saw the immense opportunity of the time; and living in an age when prelates were humbled, and armies were awed, before the impalpable power of Rome, without helmet or mitre he stood invincible for pure freedom of soul.

He was equally great in intellectual force, and in the more vital and sovereign energy of character and will. His whole personality went into his work, with an utter consecration. It was this which made him so momentous a force in the great discussion and stir of his time. It was this which set him in living fellowship with great souls of the past. It was not Bradwardine, or Grostête, alone, whom he represented. The freedom-loving archbishops of England had in him an unprelatical successor. Augustine, Bernard, Thomas Aquinas, Peter Lombard, their thought he had mastered, and wherever their spirit had been most royal he also had felt it. Even Dominic and Francis had given to him of the fire of their souls.* The Saxon Church found in this priest of Norman descent the sympathizing champion of its long-struggling and unsatisfied zeal. So his life had the roots, and his influence took the reach, which transcend the limitations of individual force, which belong to essential moral powers, successively impersonated, never destroyed, and at home in all ages.

The years which followed him in his own country were years of darkness, almost of death, to the cause with which he identified his life. Almost singly, for a time, he had held antagonist forces at bay. With the withdrawal of his grand personality, the powers which he had arrested for the time gained volume and velocity, while they learned a new cruelty both from previous fear and from later success. His followers were scattered, and multitudes of them were ruthlessly flung to the flood or the flame. In the Convocation of A.D. 1408, it was forbidden to translate the Scriptures or to read any version of them composed in his time.† After the Council of Constance, by which all

---

* "In one passage he even places St. Francis of Assisi with his mendicancy, side by side with the Apostles Peter and Paul, with their hard labor. . . . . And in other places he expresses himself in such terms as to show that he looks upon the foundations, both of St. Francis and St. Dominic, as a species of reformation of the Church, yea, as a thought inspired by the Holy Ghost himself."—*Lechler*, "*John Wiclif*," etc., Vol II., p. 143.

† "Therefore we enact and ordain that no one henceforth do, by his own authority, translate any text of Holy Scripture into the English

his writings were condemned, his bones were burned, and their very ashes strewed on the stream, that Avon might carry them to Severn, and Severn to the sea; but it was, as his disciples said, that the World might be his sepulchre, and Christendom his convert. There came a time, even in England, when the fatal laws against his adherents fell dead in their places, and when the almost anarchic frenzy which attended the long wars of the Roses gave way to a peace in which liberty thrived. That was the time for which his quickening thought had waited; and having brooded silent in the air it then burst into voice, as if touching a thousand souls at once. Still earlier on the Continent, in Bohemia, and in Italy, had been felt his vast impulse. John Huss, Jerome of Prague, Savonarola, repeated the onset of his fearless spirit on the system which, like him, they fought to the death, with their differing powers, with their equal consecration; and no one of all died in vain.*

---

tongue, or any other, by way of book or treatise; nor let any such book or treatise now lately composed in the time of John Wycliffe, aforesaid, or since, or hereafter to be composed, be read in whole or in part in public or private, under the pain of the greater excommunication."— *Quoted by Vaughan, "Life of Wycliffe,"* Vol. II., p. 44, (note).

* "Huss himself declares, in a paper composed about the year 1411, that, for thirty years, writings of Wicklif were read at Prague University, and that he himself had been in the habit of reading them for more than twenty years."—*Neander, "Hist. of Church,"* Vol. V., p. 242.

The Roman Catholic Lingard says of him : " Wycliffe made a new translation, multiplied the copies with the aid of transcribers, and by his poor

In a copy of the Missal containing the ancient Hussite Liturgy, in the library of the "Clementinum" at Prague, richly illuminated by loving hands, Wycliffe is pictured at the top, lighting a spark; Huss, below him, blowing it to a flame; Luther, still lower, waving on high the lighted torch. It is a true picture of that succession in which others followed, with brightening lustre, this "Morning Star of the Reformation," till the sky was glowing, through all its arch, with the radiance of the up-springing light!

Out of that Reformation issued the new prophetic age whose ample brightness is around us. It lifted England to its great place in Europe. It wrenched powerful states from the Papal control. It gave a wholly new freedom to spirit and thought. It filled this land with its Protestant colonies. It opens to us opportunity and hope. It is on the work accomplished by Wycliffe, and by those who followed, that our liberties have been builded. They are not accidental. They have not been based on diplomacies, or on battles, however these may have sometimes confirmed them. They have not been framed, in their

---

priests recommended it to the perusal of their hearers. In their hands it became an engine of wonderful power. Men were flattered by the appeal to their private judgment; its new doctrines insensibly gained partisans and protectors in the higher classes, who alone were acquainted with the use of letters; a spirit of inquiry was generated; and the seeds were sown of that religious revolution which in little more than a century astonished and convulsed the nations of Europe."—*Hist. of Eng.*, Vol. III., p. 311.

solid strength, by the theories of philosophers, or the inventive devices of statesmen. They are founded on the Bible, made common to all. They have been wrought to their vast, enduring, symmetrical proportions—more lovely than of palaces, statelier than cathedrals—by their wisdom and patience who had learned from the Bible that human power has no authority over the conscience; that man, through Christ, has inheritance in God; and that, by reason of his immortality, he has a right to be helped, and not hindered, by the Government which is the organ of society. If the England of Victoria is different from that of Richard Second, if the present Archbishop of Canterbury is a holy apostle by the side of Courtenay or Arundel, if the story of what the kingdom then was appears to men now a ghastly dream—it is because the Bible was made, through toil, and strife, and agony of blood, the common possession of the people who dwelt "on the sides of the North."*

Thank God! that the Book, which at Oxford and Lutterworth was first transferred, in its whole extent, to the English tongue, which this Society has so widely distributed, and for whose final revised trans-

---

* "Almost a hundred and fifty years before Luther, nearly the same doctrines as he taught had been maintained by Wyckliffe, whose disciples, usually called Lollards, lasted as a numerous, though obscure and proscribed sect, till, aided by the confluence of foreign streams, they swelled into the Protestant Church of England."—*Hallam*, "*Const. Hist. of Eng.*," Vol. I., p. 57.

lation we now are looking, has been, is now, and shall be henceforth, the American Inheritance: expounded from the pulpit, taught in the household, at home in the school. It is not ours by our own effort, but by this struggle of many generations. It is not ours for our own time alone, but for the centuries which shall follow. The half-millennium which has passed since Wycliffe, the millennium since Alfred founded his "Dooms" on its Commandments, have not wasted its force. With a Divine energy it works to-day, on every hand, for grace and greatness. No future age will cease to need its law, and truth, and inspiration.

To us is given the humbler work of making it general and permanent in the land, as others for us have made it free. In the measure of our indebtedness to them, are we responsible for this future. Let us not be unmindful of the great obligation! Let us rival, at least, their zeal for freedom, their devotion to truth, if we may not rival that invincible courage which shrank not from prisons, and was friendly with Death: that these our years of noisy whirl may have in them still the moral forces which gave to theirs majestic renown; that the frame of free government, and of spiritual worship, builded on their immortal foundations, may be worthy the grand and costly life which cemented its base; that the latest age of American History still may repeat those words of Wycliffe, written amid the heavy glooms which now are scattered, and in the front of menacing perils which now are not: "I am assured that the Truth of the Gospel may, indeed, for a time, be cast down in particular places, and may, for a while, abide in silence, in consequence of the threats of Antichrist; but extinguished it never can be. For the Truth itself has said, "Heaven and earth shall pass away, but my words shall never pass"!

www.ingramcontent.com/pod-product-compliance
Lightning Source LLC
Chambersburg PA
CBHW020325090426
42735CB00009B/1405